do you know me?

DREAMING AGAINST THE ODDS
IN AN AMERICAN CITY

by

Hillari Fine Sasse
& the kids

PHOTOGRAPHY BY KATHY KJAR

EDITED BY SUSAN CAVITCH

GUILD BINDERY PRESS, MEMPHIS TENNESSEE

do you know me?

by Hillari Fine Sasse & the kids

P H O T O G R A P H Y   B Y   K A T H Y   K J A R

Published in Memphis, Tennessee by Guild Bindery Press, Inc.

Library of Congress Cataloging-in-Publication Data

LC Card Catalog Number 94-78029

Editor and Publisher: Randall Bedwell
Senior Editor: Robbin Brent
Associate Editors: Palmer Jones, Trent Booker
Consulting Editor: David Yawn
Production Manager / Design: Pat Patterson, Patterson Design Works
Production Assistant: Greg Hastings
Public Relations: Virginia Davis
Volunteer Coordinator: Renee Fernandez

Sasse, Hillari Fine
<u>do you know me? dreaming against the odds in an American city</u>

Kathy Kjar, Photographer
Paula Greenberg, Art Director

ISBN # 1-55793-024-4

Urban Anthropology / Children's issues

published in the United States by

Guild Bindery Press, Inc.
Post Office Box 38099
Memphis, Tennessee 38183

Printed by Wilson Graphics, Memphis, Tennessee
Softbound by Southern Bindery, Memphis, Tennessee

1 2 3 4 5 6 7 8 9 10
First Edition

Royalties from the sale of this book will go directly to stand by me, inc., an all-volunteer nonprofit agency that supports homeless children.

self-portrait by Tangi

We would like to thank the following corporations, individuals and churches who purchased advance copies of do you know me?

Promus Companies
Federal Express
Methodist Health Systems
Steak Out
Solomon Schechter Day School
The Kroger Company
St. Joseph's Hospital
Davis Kidd Booksellers
The Deliberate Literate
Poag and McEwen
The University of Memphis
Barnes and Nobles/Bookstar
C. Suzanne Landers and Laurel Reisman
Memphis and Shelby Co. Public Library
First United Methodist Church
Final Net, Inc.
St. John's United Methodist Church
Calvary Episcopal Church
Robbin Brent
Blue Cross/Blue Shield of Memphis, Inc.
South Central Bell
M.S. Carriers
John and Palmer Jones
Backstreet Couriers, Inc.
Commissioner and Mrs. Edward F. Williams III
Virginia Davis
Mike Roberts, Attorney at Law
Delta Airlines
WREG TV
WREC-AM/WEGR-FM/96 X-FM
Crye Leike, Inc.
Northwestern Mutual Life
State Farm Insurance
United Way of the Mid-South
Langston Companies
Time Warner/Cablevision
Regency Travel
Leader Federal Bank for Savings
WPTY-TV/WLMT-TV
Nationwide Insurance
Arbonne
Mr. and Mrs. Walker Uhlhorn
Cathie Griffith/Strategic Marketing
Shelley Phillipy/One Source Marketing
George Holley Insurance Agency
Buckman Laboratories

Century 21 Action Associates
Dr. Gilbert Stein
Fernando and Renee Fernandez
J. C. Bradford and Company - Ruth Lentz
The Law Firm of Petkoff and Lancaster
Kappa Delta National Sorority - Kimberly Skinner
  and Melanie McMillan
First Federal Bank
Dr. Joel Kronenberg
Germantown Chiropractic Clinic
James E. Turner, MD, PhD
International Risk Consultants-Littleton, Colorado
Dr. and Mrs. Roy Greenberg
Shirley G. Nowalsky
Lawyers Title Insurance Corporation
  Michael Fearnley and Employees
Henry Halle, III
The Don Hutson Organizations

TABLE OF CONTENTS

I read children's books about children or books written to children all of the time. And that's exactly what they are. I have never read stories told by children which have such far-reaching implications.

This book depicts the pain of children, the suffering, and some of the joy expressed in their community. Yet it offers hope because these children have their own hopes and dreams of what the future could hold for them.

Someone else looking at an object could tell you that it is beautiful, but you may not know all of the beauty until you see it with your own eyes. These children show us the ugliness and the beauty of life through their own eyes.

I believe this book will help us to understand what it is we need to be about when it comes to the needs of the young in our universe.

—JoeAnn Ballard

I N T R O D U C T I O N

V. Lane Rawlins, President
The University of Memphis

The very idea of homeless children tugs at my heart and pricks my conscience. Who are these children and why are they homeless? How do they live, how are they affected and how will this background shape their future? The experience of inner-city children is of great concern to all of us, not only because we should care about any who are in need or whose development may be stunted but also because, in this generation, there are so many who share these conditions that it directly influences our lives and the lives of our families.

Hillari Sasse and "the kids", supported by the beautiful photography of Kathy Kjar, helps us to understand that homeless and other inner-city children are very much like our own children and grandchildren. They have a zest for living and learning that shows in their stories, pictures and poems; and they desperately want to impress their peers and find a social place where they can be noticed and accepted. Like children everywhere, they look to adults as their role models, and their vision of the future is usually formed around an adult that they admire. As I read through this book and studied the drawings and photos, I had a growing feeling that the imaginations of these children were greater and more expansive than those in a more affluent and safer setting. Perhaps an abundant imagination is necessary to compensate for impoverished circumstances.

While they are beautiful and hopeful, these kids show the damaging effects of where and how they live; they have to cope with things that those in more comfortable circumstances are spared. What shows through dramatically is the insecurity and uncertainty about what tomorrow will bring or, in the case of some of the older children, whether or not there will be a tomorrow. They write and talk openly about personal experiences with fighting and other violence that goes far beyond the experiences of most adults in our society. These children have seen how drugs destroy lives even while they bring much-needed money into the community. Thus, their lives are filled with mixed signals, a confusion of vastly different but successful adult stereotypes and, most of all, fear.

The damage is not beyond repair. The children dream of stable homes in nice neighborhoods; they want to be fathers and mothers as well as doctors, teachers, architects and ballerinas. Most of all they cry out to be heard, seen and just to be somebody that the rest of the world will recognize and appreciate. I understand all these things for they are like my own children and grandchildren—they are like me!

Hillari Sasse is obviously a dedicated, talented and generous person who developed this book as an extension of her love for the children and her hope that she can help some of them by increasing our understanding and awareness. This book made me want to do something, and I know from long-standing experience that the best thing I can do with such a feeling is to work it off. I hope it affects you that way. That is what Hillari wants and what these children, and many others like them, need. So, if you are as touched as I am, please go all the way to the back of the book and look for the list of opportunities as "a place to start."

Acknowledgements

For the vast majority, the sum total of life will be the people we have known, and more particularly, the people we have loved.

—John Henry Newman

I want to thank the women who helped make this book a reality. Kathy Kjar, a talented photographer, was my partner, my confidant, and will always be my dear friend. She shared my vision, saw the possibilities and helped me follow their lead. Susan Cavitch was my strength. She nurtured me through the difficult process of maintaining the integrity of each child's words. Her influence touched each page, as well as my life. Paula Greenberg is a unique blend of creative energy and a heart of gold. I had only to say, "could you ...," and Paula would answer, "yes." She inspired these children to reach, to explore and to create. She inspired me. Karen Barber opened her home to all of us. Her dedication to this project echoes her dedication to children.

I thank V. Lane Rawlins and JoeAnn Ballard for agreeing to add their visions and offering their words for this book. Dr. Stanley Hyland, chairman of the Department of Anthropology at The University of Memphis not only encouraged me to leave traditional academic avenues, he insisted. His expectations for this project set the standards of excellence we strived to maintain.

Many other individuals contributed. Some shared their talents, some their expertise, some read drafts and offered insights, some donated resources. These include Michael Fearnley, my sister, Roberta Fine, and Paula's brother, Leon Nowalsky, who contributed their legal advice and counsel. Lisa and Michael Chismark, Drs. Jaqueline Hecht and Wayne Dorris, Steve Cutler, John Lester, Marti Esplin, Troy Gafford, Barbara Jimenez, Shelley Lowell, Barbara Ostrow, Leslie Wittmann, Dr. Joseph Hawes, Laura Ingram, Dorothy March, Matt Cavitch, Lisa Olsen and the many friends who asked, "How is the book coming?" and stayed around to listen to the often long-winded response.

A special thanks is extended to Pam Pederson, a gifted and willing teacher, Linda Williams, whose belief in the project took it to a new level, Lori McEwen's creative and insightful voice, Gerald Montgomery, Robert Kerr for his supportive article, Dr. Ramsey Fowler for his encouragement and Ginny Davis and Renee Fernandez for their enthusiasm.

And an additional thank you must be extended to Alex Kotlowitz, author of the 1991 book, <u>There Are No Children Here</u>. My husband read this book, then gave it to me—I then gave it to Lisa. This was our "place to start."

Another thank you to Dr. Tom Wilson and Tracy Silver for their continuing support, and Randall Bedwell and his team at Guild Bindery Press: Margot McNeely, Robbin Brent, Pat Patterson, Greg Hastings and Palmer Jones. Their talents and dedication to this project made our vision a reality.

A hug and thank you to my parents, Herman and Mildred Fine for their weekly phone calls, constant encouragement, and childhood lesson that children everywhere have unlimited potential. An additional thank you goes to Maria and Winfried Sasse.

Kathy thanks her parents, Ken and Rene Chidester, and sister, Raynee Bengtzen, for their love and support. She also thanks Steve and Marcia Bean for their faith and encouragement, and Elaine Tanner, Carol Burns and the people at American Camera.

Paula would like to thank her parents, Harry and Shirley Nowalsky for their love, support, patience, and guidance. Their lifelong example of honesty and their sense of community have proven to be a source of great inspiration. And to her sister, Judy, a special thank you for always being there.

Kathy, Paula and I would like to thank our husbands, Jeff, Roy and Michael for their guidance and cooking abilities. Also, we thank our daughters for the life lessons and the love.

And finally, thank you to the children and their families for sharing their words, wisdom, experiences, art and poetry. They will forever remind us that one person can significantly enhance the life of another.

Author's Note

The following pages chronicle the thoughts, hopes and fears of a group of homeless and inner-city children. Surrounded by violence and poverty, these children still continue to dream. They have managed to retain a courage, and a willingness, to love, to forgive and to endure. Most will have to fight the odds to obtain an adequate education. Some will reach their potential, some will not.

Many of these children are registered with Final Net, a homeless children's program established by Dr. Tom Wilson and Karen Barber in Memphis, Tennessee. Photographer Kathy Kjar, art instructor Paula Greenberg and I met them while serving as community volunteers. We listened as they told us about their lives and their circumstances. We danced to their music, ate cheeseburgers and Twinkies and held their hands in the rain while walking them home.

Those interactions became this book's heart and soul. During that time, we interviewed, photographed, drew, painted and colored with more than twenty homeless and previously homeless children. Many of our workshops were so emotional that the adults participating would have to step out, regroup, then calmly re-renter the room. Many times we laughed so hard that working was out of the question; we had gone over the edge.

Often the children would take off into outbursts of sheer absurdity, far from the focus of the sessions. We gladly indulged them in these episodes. Yet, always, somewhere, reality would re-enter the dialogue, and we would remember our purpose. We were there to be educated, and then to attempt to educate.

These children want a chance. They want their art, their experiences and their wisdom to motivate others. They want to be heard. This book is their voice.

art by Gabriel

hey Miss Hillari, guesswhat I did today!

art by LaToya

the big cheese

the big cheese

*"Osha came knockin' on my front door. She said
the big cheese was coming at 5:30."*

❦

They call her "the big cheese." She's an old, broken-down white and green church bus covered with rust spots. The rust spots give her an animated look—like an enormous piece of Swiss cheese. She was a gift to Final Net, and the children love her.

Gerald, the driver of the big cheese, travels the inner-city neighborhoods in search of homeless and previously home-less children. He knows where to look. Together, Gerald and the cheese collect more than sixty children from various shelters and emergency housing projects in the Memphis area. Even those who leave the shelters and move on are found. The children can count on that.

"I was puzzled that the big cheese wasn't going to come. [And then] when I saw that long white and green bus, then I jumped up and down and wasn't sad."

The children look for the cheese. They listen for her. They wonder when she will come; they cry if she doesn't, and they leap with delight when she does. Though in constant need of repairs, the cheese endures. Gerald's creative mechanics and the children's prayers keep her running.

Gerald, picture by Terri

8

Tamika

Gerald drives the bus because he cares about the children. He likes to watch their faces light up when he turns the corner, and he likes to make a difference in their lives.

"They don't want to go back. They're just having fun and all. I let them make loud noises; you know, it's the best time they've had. When they get home, they got to stay in the house; so when they get with *me, boy, it's the best thing that ever happened. That's the reason I like the children. They get a chance to go out, eat and play and have some things. It's real nice. Some of them want to go home with me, but I can't carry them home. They know I'm not going to let nothing happen to them."*

The cheese doesn't just represent a destination. She has become the matriarch of a band of children. Within her doors is a community they can call their own. They don't notice her torn upholstery and sticking windows; they only see their friends.

The cheese offers them a continuity that is lacking in their transient lives. Change is their reality. They change shelters, houses and schools. Often they live temporarily with extended family. Despite all this, the cheese is constant. She picks them up for tutoring, for Saturday activities and for adventures down winding country roads leading to Miss Karen's farm.

James

the big cheese, by Cori

Raymond, Cori and Gregory

Osha

But Gerald and the cheese have taken the children through war zones as well as down country roads.

"The bus came 'round the corner and took off ['cause they were] shooting across the street."

Gerald hit the gas and the children hit the floor. The shooting was unrelated to the traveling bus, but when the children heard the familiar echo of gunshots, they knew instinctively what to do. "I laid down on the floor of the bus," LaToya later explained. The children huddled together on the floor of the cheese while Gerald maneuvered them to a safer area.

"Everybody was scared and still down on the floor. I told them to stay down there, and I was ducking, too. I almost hit a few cars. I was that scared. It was better to hit a car than a kid. If he had shot straight where I was going, he would have shot straight through the middle of the bus. He would have got somebody."

self-portrait by Terri

I don't want a sofa

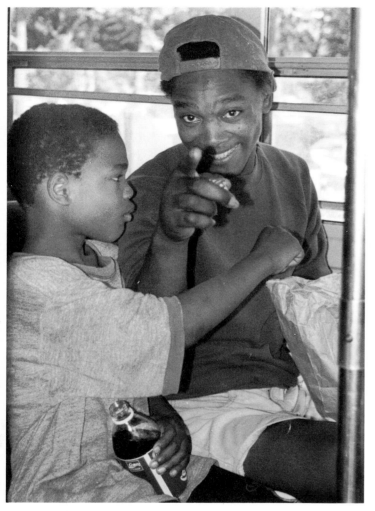

I noticed him immediately. He stood near the rear of the Final Net project room and watched as his son, Raymond Jr., was greeted affectionately by a young volunteer. His three children had told him about the big cheese. They told him about the activities and the friendly people who gave them food and hugs and encouragement. Raymond wanted to see more; he wanted his family to be a part of something good.

Raymond and son, Raymond Jr.

Raymond and Gerald

He began by riding on the cheese. He met Gerald—the children's driver, protector and friend. Almost immediately, Raymond felt the atmosphere of anticipation and warmth that his children had described.

Raymond's manner is somewhat shy, but he smiles easily and often. In his reversed baseball cap and baggy blue jean shorts, he looks much younger than twenty-eight. He and his family live in a housing project in South Memphis. Every day he walks his children to a school located just outside the boundaries of their neighborhood. He hasn't had permanent employment since an injury on the job last year, so he works doing whatever he can, whenever he can. Raymond's family was homeless. Now this is their home.

I began to see Raymond whenever I was with the children. Sometimes we talked about Raymond Jr.'s contribution to this book, and sometimes we just passed the time. When I asked him if he'd like to share some of his thoughts about homelessness and his children, he laughed and wondered what he could say that I could put in a book. He would be surprised.

"Last Saturday, this guy knocked on the door here—I had seen him before—said he was dodging from his wife, could he come to sit down. Come to find out he robbed the school. In order for them [the children] to thrive, they got to be in a better environment. This is not a good environment.

"I'm not scared living here. I was when I first got here, but you just have to [tell] yourself to stay out of other people's business and nobody gets in your business. So you just train yourself to live in this environment.

"They tell me that I can't go to another program. I would like to have a section eight home. I would like to have a home. Not this kind of environment, 'cause this is just too many people here, and it's just wild. There's no respect."

Gabriel, LaTosha, Tangi, Michael

15

*"They stole a television.
They take groceries too."*

Gerald became our self-appointed chaperone on trips to the inner-city's shelters and housing projects.

"I'll take you to Fowler; that's no place for you two alone."

He transported Kathy and me on the cheese and expertly, if somewhat anxiously, guided us through various sections of downtown Memphis. During one excursion to Raymond's apartment, the bus lost its brakes. Groceries we had purchased flew everywhere.

When we arrived at our destination, we faced another tense situation. There had been a shooting, and the crowd and police had scattered just minutes before. The stress was still evident. Nerves were raw. Raymond was concerned for our safety and suggested that Kathy confine her photography to the area just outside his front door, while he and I conducted our interview away from the covered window. I sat on the floor.

Our interview proceeded quietly, but Kathy and her camera equipment were far too tempting a distraction to remain inconspicuous. Within minutes, she was surrounded by children eager to investigate. Simply by entering Raymond's apartment with groceries and camera equipment, we unknowingly targeted his home.

"[I've] been broken in. I got a sheet from the policeman I'm supposed to fill out and send back today. They stole a television. They take groceries too. Anytime you bring something into your apartment, you're at risk. You've already been seen."

Raymond's apartment

I don't want a sofa

Raymond's apartment was proof of his concerns. His unit had no carpet, no curtains and no pictures on the wall. Bed sheets covered the windows, and the one sofa was worn and broken. A shabby television set—a replacement for the one that was stolen—sat on the floor directly across from the couch. There were no amenities, and barely the necessities. When we suggested that Raymond contact some agencies to refurnish his apartment, he was afraid of the attention that acquiring even basic household items would receive. He didn't want a sofa. Emptiness represented security.

❧

Quinton

"The way we're living now, I'm sorry,

but I can't do any better."

Raymond's love for his children is not reflected in their appearance or their home. Their surroundings are neglected; their clothes are usually ragged and worn. Raymond reluctantly accepts his family's circumstances, but he still hangs on to some hope for his children's future.

"I remember not wanting kids. I remember not wanting them at all, 'cause I come out from a family of thirteen, and all the problems that we had to go through. I didn't want no children. I didn't want them to go through [what I did].

[But] from watching that child born, it was like a miracle, and it was just —I don't know—just something that filled me inside, and I fell in love with that child. I didn't want it at first, but when it got here, I fell in love. And if I had to do [it] over again, I'd do it again. I'd rather have the child than not to have one, 'cause being by yourself, I don't want to be by myself. I wouldn't want to do without them."

Often he defines their lives in terms of what they do not have.

"What I try to teach my children is I try to tell them, 'The way we're living now, I'm sorry, but I can't do any better. I can't find a good job. But it's going to be alright. I wish I could put you all through college. Keep your grades up and maybe you'll go somewhere. They just brought some certificates home yesterday, the Principal's Honor Roll. I told them I was going to hang them and get some frames for them. I try to make them keep their grades up."

Tangi lives in the same South Memphis
housing project as Raymond and his children.
Unlike Raymond's children, Tangi walks
thirty minutes to her school each morning.
She does not walk down tree-lined streets; she
walks through neighboring projects where she
is considered a trespasser by the resident
teen-agers. Every day Tangi is afraid, and
every day she takes a chance.

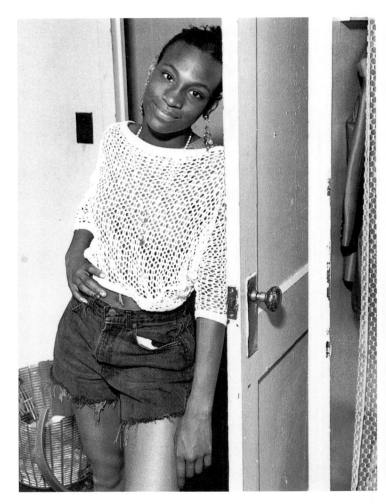

Tangi

"What it is, it's this project thing they've started. If you're not from the project—like if I live in Fowler Homes and I'm walking through Clayburn—the group's going to jump me. They say, 'You're violating our property.'"

Tangi is long and lean with a generous smile. She has an air of drama about her and will occasionally begin to sing mid-sentence. She is thirteen and beautiful. But being beautiful where Tangi lives doesn't make life easy. She has good reason to be afraid. Men often pay too much attention to her.

While homeless and sheltered in emergency housing, Tangi was molested. She knew the two men. One was the brother of an aquaintance. The police asked a lot of uncomfortable questions and then apprehended one man. The other lives in a housing project Tangi must walk through every day on her way to school.

"He's still out. I'm kind of afraid because he's supposed to be staying at Clayburn Homes—very near me. I have to walk to school past there. My mom was trying to get the school bus for us, but they wouldn't accept things. We sent [a petition] to the board. They rejected it, so I'm still walking."

Tangi doesn't hesitate when asked what scares her the most about her walks to and from school.

"When men are out. One man my mom had to talk to because he was getting in my face walking home from school. He hasn't messed with me since."

23

Michael

LaTosha

Fowler Homes, Memphis, Tennessee

Tangi's younger sister and brother go to a closer school. They're not afraid of the walk; they're afraid of the gunshots and the night. Ten-year-old LaTosha and eight-year-old Michael usually find their mother's bed when the nighttime shooting gets too loud or too close.

"One time they were shooting, and me and my brother woke up. We went in on the couch where my mother was sleeping. We didn't go back to bed. I stayed up all night and I fell asleep in school."

Guns, drug dealers and anger; these are the enemies, the real-life monsters these children must keep at bay each day. They laugh, they play and they endure. Slowly this endurance turns into a facade of indifference. They refer almost off handedly to the violence in their own neighborhoods.

"The only thing I can say about [Dixie] emergency housing is they find a decent time to do something— when everybody is awake, before you go to sleep at night. That's how I like it. Do all you're going to do during the daytime; don't wait until nighttime."

"I don't like it at all," adds twelve-year-old Gabriel.

The children know what they want to say; we don't need to ask. We listen as they describe their fears.

"I be scared when people be walking behind you, and they're looking at you. You think they be staring at you, and they going to do something to you."

"When it's dark, go inside.

Don't never come out of the door."

"I'm scared [walking home from school] 'cause there be drug dealers right beside you."

*"Some children that come to school, they be fighting all the time and pushing people down.
They always fight."*

*"At my school, I saw this little girl get shot. I went to the assistant principal [and told them]
they shot her in the hand."*

**Every one of these children has seen someone shot, not just on TV but in real life.
They each have a story to tell.**

"I saw a man shot in the leg; he was laying on the ground. We walked past him."

"If I see someone shooting, I'm not going to tell 'cause they might come shoot me."

"Yeah, they'd come looking for you."

*"In Hurt Village there were these two boys. They tried to beat up my brother, and he ran in the house,
and my momma closed the door just in time 'cause there were three bullet holes in the door."*

"When it's dark, go inside. Don't never come out of the door."

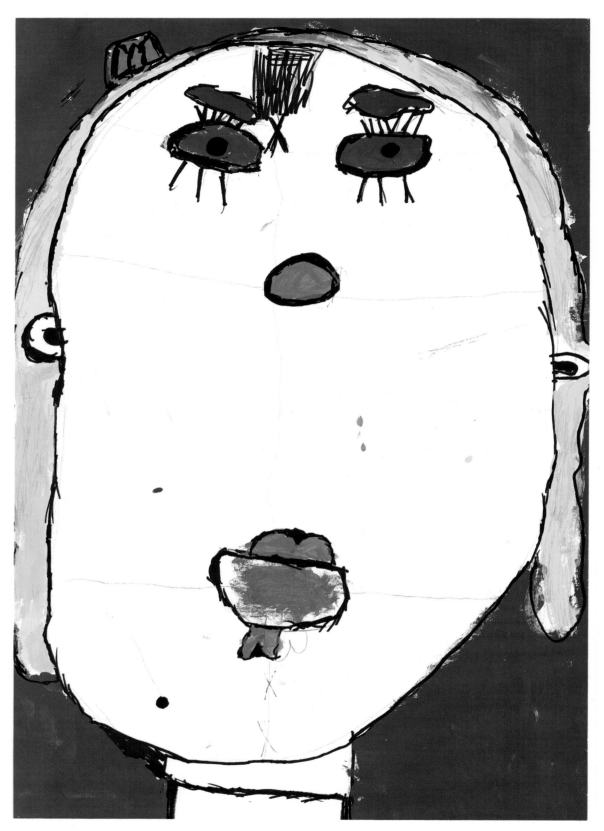

art by Cori

castles in the sky

"*This is the balcony*

if I want to go up and see the sky."

Raymond doesn't want a sofa. Tangi doesn't want to walk to school. LaTosha doesn't want to sleep alone at night, and LaToya doesn't want to talk about it. In order to survive, these children must find ways to hide their fears. They don't talk about violence when they play; they create magic with whatever resources are available. Their art, their poetry, their music and their imaginations allow them to enter worlds otherwise unknown to them. These children are still young enough to dream.

Homeless children dream of homes. Some of their fantasies are vivid and detailed. Some simply describe a place with a backyard, lots of windows and a permanent address. Yet even their simplest dreams remain far from their realities. They live in shelters. Some live in the Memphis Housing Authority (MHA) emergency units, some in Metropolitan Inter-Faith Association (MIFA) emergency homes, and some have spent more time than they should in daily shelters just to escape the streets.

Osha imagines a house with balconies, a pool and fountains. Her two children could play in the treehouse. Osha has designed a castle in the sky.

&

"This is the playground for my children, and this is the balcony if I want to go up and see the sky. This is the hole in the tree so the children can go up and play. This is the fountain and this is the swing on the porch. And this is another balcony. She [the girl in the picture] is looking at the sky and surroundings—grass and everything."

Stephanie and Osha

Stephanie and Osha want to be together always. They are cousins who share the dream of living in houses with backyards and room to grow. They'll live next door and be friends forever. Stephanie has a definite picture of her future home.

art by Stephanie

"This is my house I just bought. I live in the number one house.

This is my car, and my two children are in it. Bushes are around the house,

and [it has] colorful windows. They have stars on the windows like in a church.

In the back of my house, I have a pool. It is in the country."

art by Michael

Tangi, LaTosha and Michael share images of their dream homes. Michael wants vivid colors and designs.

"Designs on the door, designs and colors on the chimney, gate and grass. My sign says, 'Come in.' Designs mean that I want to make it look wonderful."

Michael

LaTosha

LaTosha's plans are full of detail.

art by LaTosha

"This is my pool. I have a Jacuzzi inside; you can take a bath

or hot tub. This is an apple tree and a peach tree. This will be a

garden with lettuce, tomatoes, carrots, beets and watermelon.

This is my room, and this is my friend's room. This is when I go to college.

This is a double door. One side opens, the other doesn't.

I have a chimney in my house. It's in St. Louis."

art by Tangi

Tangi

Tangi worries about safety. Security cameras surround her dream home.

"You can have a camera with all these TVs on the inside.

A front door camera, you look at the TV and see who's there."

art by Gregory

Gregory

Gregory is practical.

"So many windows and doors.

In case of fire you can jump out."

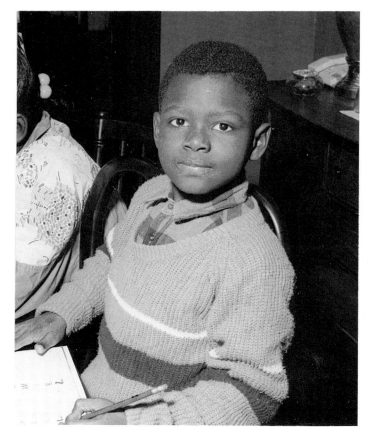

James

James's home has room for all.

art by James

"There are fences so my dogs won't get out.

One is a puppy. [In my room is] a bed, a carpet.

It's blue and the curtains are green."

LaToya's images are darkened by the reality of where and how she lives today. She doesn't fantasize about style or color or design, she dreams about the very concept of having a home. LaToya begins her story by detailing pleasant images of her grandfather's farm, then she abruptly refocuses her thoughts on the harsh realities in her life.

LaToya

art by LaToya

"This is my house, a little pond and some flowers. Windows with zigzags on them. My daddy lives on a farm in Tunica; my granddaddy's on a farm. He has chickens and chicks. I'm going this summer—Dixie [housing] is bad. They begin shooting every night, and one little girl, she got run over. I get under the bed at night. This man was shot in the arm, and he run up the steps where we stayed and got onto the building and jumped. One man was in the middle of the street, and he stabbed himself ten times."

art by Tangi

when my
nose be
itching

art by Stephanie

"[I'm happy on] my birthday. I'll be twelve.

When I get money from my momma and I go to the store.

I like to spend and save." —Stephanie

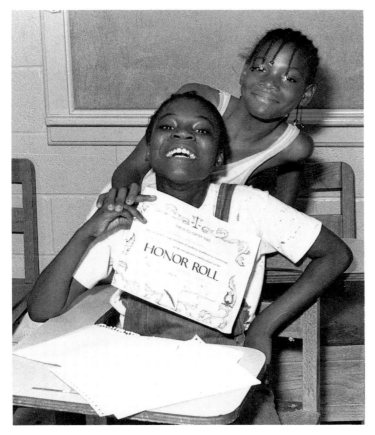

LaTosha and Naomi

Tangi wants to talk first, but Cori won't let her. They both love to tell their stories; they both love the attention. This time Cori is faster and louder.

"I was excited 'cause I was coming over here."

"Yeah, she was jumping all around saying, 'When's the bus coming?'"

The children are talking about their emotions by sharing stories of their lives.

"[I'm happy] when I be home with my momma and my little sister and them come over. Only on Fridays we get to see them," says Terry.

Adds LaTosha, *"When I make good grades at school. I make the honor roll."*

Nature's Best

I sit and wonder about nature's best, somehow it's not like the rest. The wonderful fragrance of roses in the air, like the birds in the sky, flying where they do not know in their minds, but in their hearts they know. I guess that Mother Nature planned by the grace of GOD. He wraps his wings so tightly around me. That's what nature's all about. But there's something you should know, follow the light is where you should go.

Tangi

Tangi

Tangi finally gets her chance to talk. When Tangi tells a story, she expects everyone to listen carefully. She lowers her voice and speaks with her whole body.

"It makes me feel so good to know that I can be able to express my words, express colors and everything in the way I wanted. Because since I couldn't draw and I started writing and got a thought one day: Maybe I could express my songs in writing. It makes me happy when I sing in front of everybody—when I sit down and write a poem. Because I don't have a chance to get out all my feelings."

Then it's LaToya's turn.

"I be frightened when my nose be itching. My grandma said something be coming and that's when I put all the lights out. I be frightened; I be seeing shadows. My grandma —I sleep there sometimes 'cause she doesn't like staying by herself—my grandma opens the Bible. I sleep on the couch."

"I be frightened 'cause I see people and drug deals," **says another child,** *"and a lot of people walking around."*

"In Dixie homes I really got scared," **Tangi adds.** *"They were shooting in the apartment next to us, and it sounded like they were shooting in our bathroom. We held a match up against the window, [then] we went over to a neighbor's house."*

"Yeah, I didn't get much sleep [at Dixie]. [I was] paranoid about all the shooting," **Gabriel remembers.**

"In Dixie homes

I really got scared.

They were shooting

in the apartment next

to us, and it sounded like

they were shooting

in our bathroom."

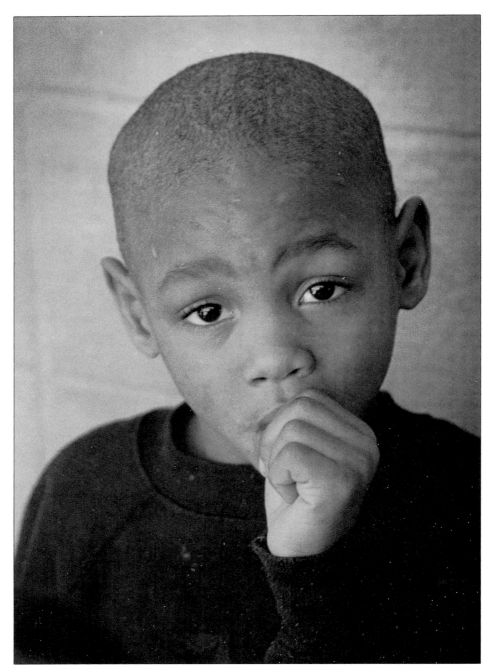

Marcus

"Some guns don't have no barrels."

The children nod their heads knowingly as others tell their stories.

"To feel safe [I would need] a security door. They be kicking in the doors, then they can't kick down the door no more."

"We would need a police officer."

"In our house we have 20 gauges, automatics and handguns."

"Yeah, a gun."

"You'd have to know how to operate it. It's hard 'cause you have to twist the barrel."

"Some guns don't have no barrels," Raymond declares. The children all agree.

"With 20 gauge you have to stop and put more bullets in. They could have done shot you by then."

Gabriel interrupts the conversation; he's had enough. He wants to think about peaceful, happy feelings. The talk of violence and guns reminds him of time spent in emergency shelters. He tries hard to forget those fears and move on.

"When you go to another school," he begins, *"and I don't know nobody at the other school, but when I go there I see another friend, you know, and then he shows me around the building and stuff. [I'm happy] when I'm going out of town to see my brother—I never get to see him. Just me and my sister live together with my grandma, and my other two brothers live with my aunty. One is eight and one is four. [I see them] every Saturday."*

Gabriel

the face is confident
kind of mad

art by Gabriel

Gabriel's smile is warm and his eyes expressive as he modestly announces to the group that he is an artist. Every night he writes and illustrates his day in a journal. Sometimes he draws fun characters; sometimes he draws what hurts. Gabriel loves the freedom, the creatiyity and the outlet his art provides. It makes him happy.

"I draw in a notebook. I like to draw Nintendo stuff. Ninja turtles too. I'd like to draw a comic book one day. I'd get excited. I started drawing when I saw my friend drawing and he said, 'Do you want to draw a comic book together?'"

Tangi ponders Gabriel's words and ends the discussion with a thoughtful twist. She describes the frustration of being old enough to know better, but too young to help.

"If you see somebody doing something wrong and you know they're from around your community, and you know you want to do something about it—especially if it's an adult. Like if you see an adult doing drugs, you really want to stop it, but you're not old enough to tell them what to do. That makes me feel hurt."

art by Terri

art by Michael

some-
body
didn't
listen

Cori

Tamika wants a good education and a better, more caring world. She hopes to fix what's wrong around her. She and the other children still believe in opportunity. We question them about their perceptions.

"[In multi-cultural class] we learn about people's lives long ago when they were fighting for freedom."

"How long ago?"

"Real long ago."

"Do you think I was born?" I asked.

"Oh no!"

"Yes, you were born before Dr. Martin Luther King."

"What did Dr. King teach?"

"Love."

"Black children and white children should be friends."

"Do you think people listened?"

"Some people, not all of them."

"One white man didn't. He shot him."

"*My name is Gregory, and my dream is*
to recycle cans and newspapers and
make the world a better place."

The children agree; somebody didn't listen. They talk about the changes that have taken place since Dr. King first shared his vision. They talk about what has come true.

"That blacks and whites will be friends. Blacks can drink out of whites' water fountains. Blacks and whites can be in the same school and go the same places."

Then they talk about what hasn't come true. Violence and drugs plague their neighborhoods, and they believe Dr. King would not have wanted it that way. They, too, have a dream.

"I have a dream. My name is Stephanie. I have a dream that everyone will stop the violence. We're brothers and sisters, and we shouldn't be fighting ... [we should be] getting along. Stop the violence, and stop killing each other—stop black on black crime. We can go to church, go to school, get an education."

"I have a dream that we stop killing each other and hurting each other, shooting everybody, and stop selling drugs."

"I have a dream that blacks and whites will communicate with each other."

"My name is Tamika, and I have a dream that more blacks will go to college than go to jail."

"My name is Gregory, and my dream is to recycle cans and newspapers and make the world a better place."

"My name is Calvin, and I have a dream that little black boys and little white boys will join hands together—and I'm glad to be black and joined hands with little white boys."

"I have a dream. I hope the world'll be a better place."

Tamika also hopes the world will be a better
place. But Tamika doesn't just hope, she con-
templates solutions. She believes that a good
education can improve the quality of a life.
She believes it can improve hers.

Tamika and Stephanie

art by Tamika

"The main thing is education. Some people say, 'I'm going to drop out and make me some money.' College, it will keep you on the straight road. A lot of people going to have to learn to work on a computer to get a job. You're going to have to have a real good education to live in the world in the near future. That's why I already started working the computers and learning more about them. 'Cause Mrs. Blake, she teaches me to work on the computer, and I'm good in math and science, and that's what's going to be important. 'Cause people are going to want to learn how to fix the ozone layer. They going to use computers in science and math, so I got a good chance of making it in the real world, 'cause I already started planning my goal and what I'm going to do."

LaToya and Cori

Homeless children's dreams are practical and passionate. They long to be someone special, to have exciting experiences, and to be happy.

"[My name is] Jevon, and I want to be a father."

"My name is Joe, and I want to be a doctor,
[and] I want to be a teacher—to help people learn."

" I want to be a football player."

"I want to be a nurse."

"I want to be an architect
so I can build houses for the homeless ...
help people get into houses."

"I want to be a ballerina."

"I want to be like Miss Karen."

art by Cori

Diane

Stephanie's dreams for the world become spoken prayers for peace. She wants life to be different, people to be different. She wants the world to care.

"People be shooting their own brothers and sisters. It's not fair. Everyone should have multi-cultural [classes] 'cause it teaches us to all get along."

Stephanie knows how to get along. She smiles a lot. She winks and skips and spreads a happy feeling. She eagerly shares her vision for the future.

"I want to be a teacher and a swimmer ... get my diploma and stay in school ... no children, but I want a husband. Oh, and my momma, buy her a house and a car and give her some money."

Diane wants to be a lawyer. If tenacity, verbal ability and charm are prerequisites, she is on her way. Her goals and spirit soar, but her resources are scarce.

"I want to be a lawyer. I want to help people solve their problems so they could tell the truth, and they don't have those problems all their lives ... so I can help people make the right decisions. I want to help mentally retarded children."

art by Osha

Osha and Terri

Osha uses her mother as inspiration.

"When I grow up, when I have some kids of my own, and I have my own good job, and my kids be in a daycare, then they be at school, and I have somewhere to stay ... [then] I'll do good things in life. I want two girls. Two because if I had one I don't want her to be bored.

"When my mom graduated from the program [at Estival Place homeless shelter] ... it's something you use to better your life. She got a certificate and she gave us a certificate. She put the certificate in a big, old frame with all the children's pictures around her picture.

"At first she didn't have much money, but after the program she started to get all kinds of jobs. She worked at Idlewild [School], and as a waitress. Now she works at the cleaners.

"My mom said she's going to get a good job and we going to move into a house 'cause of all the children. She said we might move in a building in Whitehaven. But we are still going to come here [to Final Net]."

Homeless children's dreams shatter easily. Osha's mother, Dorothea, understands this. Living takes all her energy. She stays in a homeless shelter with three of her six children. Her priority is survival. There isn't much time to encourage dreams, but Dorothea tries to remain optimistic. She clings to the hope that one day things will be different.

"[Osha] wants a lot of things I can't get her. She dreams of this mansion. She says, 'Why can't we live in a house like that?' It kind of hurts me that I can't give her the things she wants, but I'm not giving up on giving her a dream. She may be grown by the time I get it, but we'll still have it. It can be her home.

"[Osha] asks me could she take ballet lessons. I said, 'How am I going to pay for it?' You know? And with Osha's grades, I'd like to get her into an optional school. Then maybe she can work toward her goals and do some of the things she wants to do. Optional schools have music, like orchestra. At her school, they don't have nothing like that. She says, 'Momma, I want to transfer,' and I say, 'I can't just transfer you 'cause I'm on a fixed income. I can't get bus fare.' It's like she could catch the fifty and go straight up, she could catch a city bus."

Public transportation would cost around two dollars a day, five days a week, four weeks a month for just one of Dorothea's children to attend an optional school. Dorothea didn't think the optional program provided transportation. She doesn't have a car, and she doesn't have that kind of money. For her children, and for most homeless children, an optional school just isn't an option.

"A lot of parents are trying to get their kids into optional schools 'cause they have so much to offer—you know like band. They have band in elementary school. Osha went five years without having band. She probably never even played a recorder. How can they get into it in high school [when] optional kids come from elementary schools [where] they be already having training. It be something new to them. And it's hard for them just to cope with this. They be like, 'God, we know nothing about this.' They are behind everbody else; it's kind of hard."

Dorothea sees her children's education as inferior. She worked at an optional school and knows the difference. She wishes parents would fight for better schools, but she understands their limitations.

"Like from Hurt Village, kids are bused to Frayser schools. They have a parent/teacher meeting and half the parents can't go. They don't have transportation. They're not trying to get them no bus ... the bus don't go out there but two times a day, run by the school from where we live. A lot of them [the children] that go to Osha's school, their parents are on drugs, and they get themselves ready. Half of them come to school and their hair ain't combed; they ain't had a bath."

But Osha looks beyond the obstacles.

"I used to watch TV. I used to always see the ice-skating, and I like what they were doing and the different dances they were doing. I want to be an ice-skater."

"What does it take to be an ice-skater?"

"It takes a lot of practice."

"Have you ever been ice-skating?"

"No."

Osha

art by Osha

Dear Bill Clinton,

I think that if all theses old buildings be torn down and make new ones for the Homless when more people get off the street the saper our world will be.

Sincely
Cori Williams
age 11

yours truly

Dear President Clinton,

I want to tell you what I think about gays in the
military. I think gays should be in the military because they
want to be all that they could be, too. Because what if there's a
big war? If there aren't a lot of people what will we do?
If the men that are not gay doesn't want gays in the
military, well Will why don't you get a military first
for the gays? I mean you just can't just push them
off to the side. People should stop killing men that are gay
because they are people just like you and me. If you were
gay do you think that people would vote for you???
Gays also need respect they can't help that they are
gay. Their not trash you can't throw them away, and killing
them want help at all it will just make it worst.

Bye,

Jamika Davis

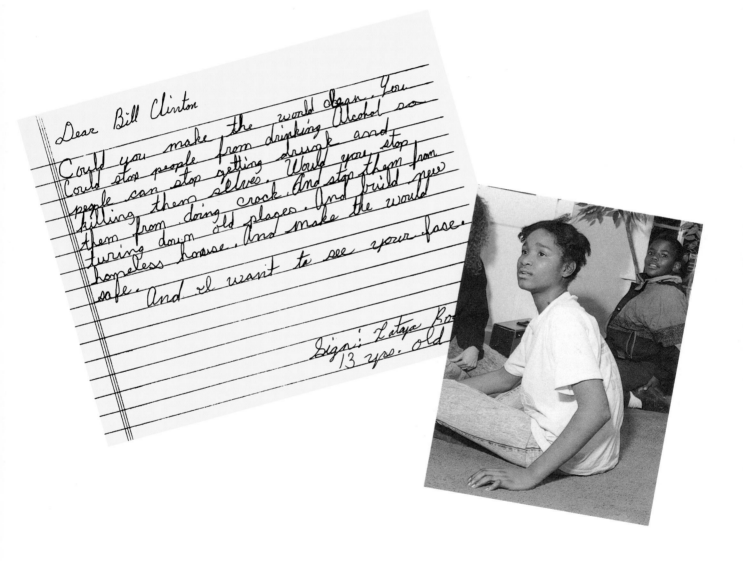

Dear Bill Clinton

Could you make the world clean. You Could stop people from drinking Alcohol so people can stop getting drunk and killing them selves. Would you stop them from doing crack. And stop them from turing down old places. And build new homeless house. And make the world safe. And I want to see your face.

Sign: Lataja Bo—
13 yrs. old

Dear President Clinton,
My name is Tangie Johnson,
and I am 10 yrs old I need to
discuss some issues with you.
The first one is I Think
children who want to sing have a
record office to go to and sign up.
THE second one is that. All
kids Should have a School bus
to ride on to be safe.

Sincerly,
Tangie

Dear Bill Cilton,

How is life going for you.
Fine I hope. MY life is going OK
I hope. MY life is going OK
you wife Hillary Cilton. Because
I want you to. The reason why I am
writing this is because I want to know
can you stop all the Violente.
I hope you can because thier is
too much around my house.
I wonder how it feel being head
of the state I would like that
one day. But what I really want
to be is a teacher. I am really looking
foward on your word. Of how to stop
Violence. Because I want your help.

Yours Truely
Stephanie
Stephanie

Bye Gregory glass
Dear Mrs. Hillary you are a lucky to have a good
little girl I hope she go to high school and
littlest girl is very quit but she is very quite
I'm Finish
Age 9 name Gregory adress 882 E. ATLa

The end

868 South 4Rth Apt. #128
Memphis, TN 38126
May 26, 1993

Dear Bill Clinton,
        You are the best president I ever
had. The day it was the vote day. Our class
voted. My teacher was the only one who
voted for George Bush. I just went to that
you for being here for all the people of
Memphis, TN.

        Yours Friend,
        Latosha Johnson

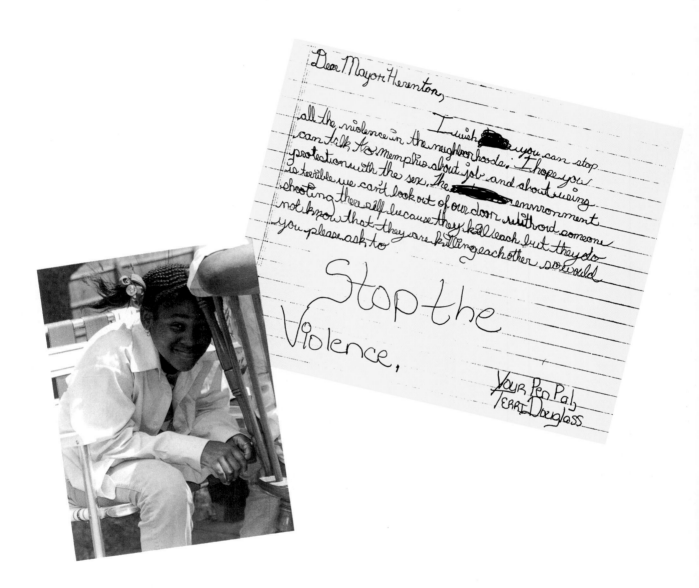

Dear Mayor Herenton,

I wish that you can stop all the violence in the neighborhoods. I hope you can talk to Memphis about job and about using protection with the sex, the environment is terrible we can't look out of our door without someone shooting there self because they kill each other but they do not know that they are killing each other so would you please ask to

Stop the Violence,

Your Pen Pal,
Terri Douglass

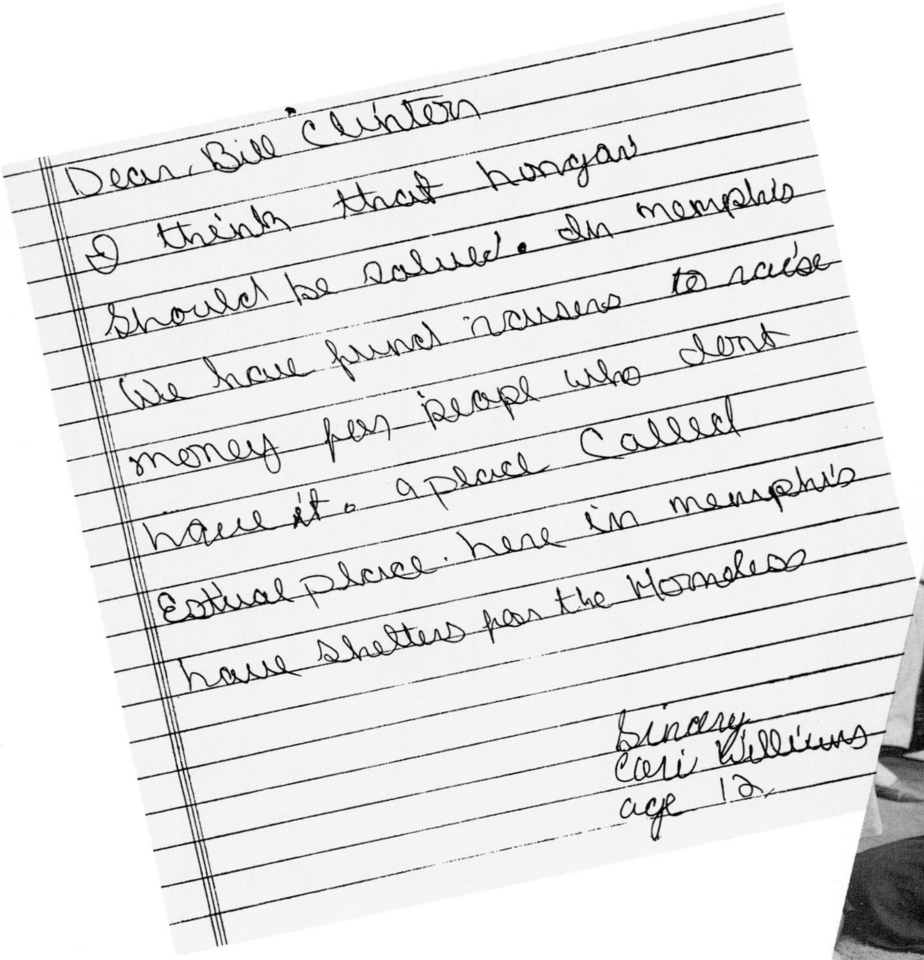

Dear Bill Clinton
I think that hungar
Should be solved. In memphis
We have fund raisers to raise
money for people who dont
have it. A place Called
Eothual place. here in memphis
have shelters for the Homeless

Sincery
Cori Williams
age 12.

87

self-portrait by Diane

one
locker
away

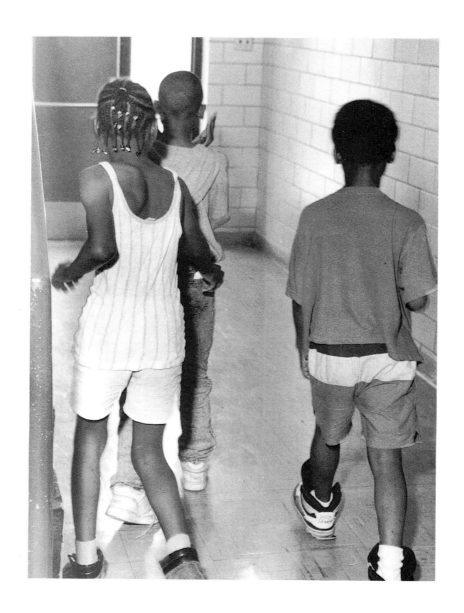

"There's a boy at our school, he brung a gun
and threatened the teacher with it."

"Some children—they be doing drugs. Yesterday when we got out of school, we went to the park, and these boys in my classroom, they were smoking, and they asked me if I wanted some, and I said no and walked away."

Ten-year-old Cori walked away, but she can't keep it out of her life. Drugs and violence are part of her daily routine.

"This boy at our school, he brung a gun and threatened the teacher with it."

"There's a boy. He said on the last day of school he was going to bring some guns."

"Our school is across from the projects, and there's a lot of boys in my school. Our teachers show them the sign on the wall: If you bring weapons or stuff or if you shoot anybody, you'll have to pay a fine. And it's a whole lot of money."

Michael

" If you were watching a fight or yelling or cheering or just walking past a fight, they could pull out a gun and shoot you right [there while they're] trying to shoot somebody else."

All of these children attend schools in the inner-city. Some will transfer numerous times before they graduate from sixth grade. Most routinely confront the dangers of the streets.

"At my school, there was one girl and another girl. One girl brung a gun, and one girl brung a knife, and they were fighting."

"[You shouldn't watch fights.] You might get hurt."

"You know whenever a fight's going, everbody wants to be around and watch the fight. If you were watching a fight or yelling or cheering or just walking past a fight, they could pull out a gun and shoot you right [there while they're] trying to shoot somebody else. [All] 'cause you were trying to watch a fight."

"At my school, everybody want to try to see fights—see who wins or lose. My principal, she said, like you would be sitting around and watching a fight and don't know who started it or why, and somebody all of a sudden pull out a gun and just start shooting, you could be shot trying to watch the fight."

Tamika

Tamika tells of danger only one locker away.

Though only a second grader, James is

not surprised by her story.

"There was this girl. She got picked up not too long ago, and she had two knives, and she was with me almost all day, and I didn't notice. She had two knives, one knife on this side and one knife on this side, and she took them to gym with her, and we had to dress out. And I noticed she was doing this: She sort of wrapped her clothes around her and pushed them up and wrapped them and put them in her locker. I said, 'What are you doing?' She didn't say anything, then she got in a fight and pulled out two knives."

At thirteen, Tamika deals with the consequences of drug abuse, violence and the escalating rate of teen pregnancy in her school. She has witnessed the repercussions.

"Not too long ago, these [two] girls were pregnant by the same boy. They weren't big; they were just pregnant, you know. One was thirteen years old. The other one, she was in eighth grade. I forgot how old she was. They started fussing, and they hit each other in the stomach, and the girl fell, and the one started stomping on her [stomach]. A lot of girls at my school are pregnant."

The children expect to see weapons at school. Regardless of their ages, they can describe in detail the pervasive violence and drug abuse.

Osha saw the number of weapons at her school drop when the menacing sixth graders graduated.

"They had a lot of [weapons] last year when the big sixth graders were there, but they left now. Last year they carried a lot of guns to school. We had a lot of police officers at our school."

school grounds

Terri and Osha

James knows far too much about violence for a child of any age.

"There's this girl, she said she had a knife. She said she want to cut Avery's heart out."

"How old is Avery?"

"Seven."

"How old is the girl?"

"Seven. She bad, too."

"Do you see weapons?"

"I seen [them] in the parking lot before. I seen [them] in a girl's locker. She put it in her book."

Raymond

Raymond, a third grader, recalls another episode.

"We heard at our school that this boy came up behind this girl and burned her hair. She had long hair and he burned it."

Many of these children walk home from school. Their paths bring them face to face with the cruelty of inner-city neighborhoods.

"When I went to my other school, there was a boy in our class—I can't remember his name. Well, he was walking home from school, and some boy shot him in the neck with a BB gun. He had to go to the hospital."

"[This girl] was beating a girl. She had her head like this [in a headlock], and they broke it up. I was [walking] behind them 'cause she said, 'You going to get it – they going to chop you up.' I was scared. This was a girls' gang.

"They were saying, 'These gang of girls going to jump you.' You figure if you talk, you going to get in trouble. I don't say nothing. They say they going to beat [another girl] up. I just turn my head and walk away."

Ruby

Ruby in the rough

She was industrious. While the other girls made their jewelry sets for family members or friends, Ruby was thinking about the possibilities. She wondered how much she could sell the sets for on the open market. She considered fifteen dollars a fair price. The material cost would be minimal, and she could handle the labor. Ruby insisted it could be done. She had my attention.

I met Ruby during a jewelry-making workshop sponsored by a local volunteer organization, and we became friends. Ruby didn't have many friends. She was seventeen years old and living at a maternity shelter for the second time in a year and a half. She had been pregnant the first time at sixteen and chose to place her baby through adoption. This child she wanted to raise on her own.

Ruby chose not to be ignored. One way or another she wanted to be noticed. She could be incredibly charming. She was beautiful. She would laugh, tease and gently touch your arm. Yet just as quickly as she offered these gifts, she would take them away and surround herself in silence. Ruby protected herself. She was a child of the system.

The Department of Human Services raised her. They made promises: The group homes would teach her values and ethics; government agencies would help her focus on the future; the foster care system would provide a nurturing home. Ruby wondered why they lied.

Ruby bounced from group homes to runaway shelters and back to group homes. She tolerated these situations until she considered them unacceptable. Then she became unresponsive, caused trouble or ran away. Running away and living nowhere in particular were Ruby's alternatives.

"I was so bad that DSS [Department of Social Services] … they just washed their hands with me. They gave up on me."

The system had her figured out. She was trouble, she was stubborn and she was unpredictable.

But Ruby was much more. She was caring, spiritual, scared and lonely. Yet she rarely let these emotions surface. She needed to be ready to fight. Her battle was with a system she didn't trust. She resented its interference, and she was afraid of its control. The system wanted her cooperation, not her anger. It got her anger.

When Ruby got angry, she ran, she rebelled or she wrote. When she wrote, her vulnerability and frustration were painfully obvious.

Bottomless Pit 10-10-90

by Ruby

They push you off so you begin
to fall,
You're going somewhere, but
nowhere at all,
You see only dark, there is no
light,
You scream and cry, but it's
useless to fight,
The world is spinning and you
can't grab on,
Your life appears and then it's
gone,
You're filled with pain but there
is no tears,
This is the worst of all
your fears,
Knowledge just has eaten
you away,
But there's nothing to do
nor nothing to say.

103

Life has been hard for Ruby. Those with the
power to affect her future were either lacking in
dedication or exhausted by Ruby's rebellious
spirit. She wanted to be productive, be a good
mother, to write her life story, but she couldn't
get started. Too often Ruby had watched as her
idealized dreams were shattered by the reality of
her isolation. She was on her own. It was just
Ruby and her baby. She wanted to succeed and
believed it was possible. She just didn't know how.

Ruby responded with rare enthusiasm when I
offered her an opportunity to share her thoughts
on life and living. She spent weeks composing
the following letter. She may not have been
heard before, but now she had a voice.

Ruby and daughter Danielle

Ruby in the rough

Hi, I'm Ruby. I am 18 years of age. I have 2 daughters. One is 20 months and one is 6 weeks. I dropped out of school. I decided to further my education. I have been away from home since the age of 3. My mom so-called neglected me. I used to be on drugs. I've gotten drunk once. I have run away 6 times. I have 3 disorderly conduct charges. I have shaved my head on one side. I hung around with the "dirty crowd." I have had at least 6-10 suspensions in 1 year for the past 3 years in school.

Now that I have told you a little about myself, let me ask some questions.

1. Who do you think I lived with?
2. Do you think that you know me from what I've said?
3. Do you label me as a troublemaker?
4. Do you think I only care about myself?
5. Am I the type of person that you feel won't succeed in life?
6. Do you feel sorry for me?
7. Do you think I'm a low-class person?

Compare your answers with my answers.

1. I lived in D.S.S. and D.H.S. custody since the age of 3.
2. No, you don't know me, you only know of me.
3. Of course I'm not a troublemaker, I just had nothing else to do 'cause no one paid attention to me.
4. Well, 20 months ago, I made a very difficult decision to place my baby for adoption because I couldn't take care of her like a mother should. And I was thinking of her, not me!
5. It really doesn't matter what you think! I know that I'm going to succeed!
6. Just put it like this, if you feel sorry for me, then I'll start feeling sorry for myself, and I really wouldn't be able to succeed in life.
7. Low, middle or high class has nothing to do with money, it has something to do with each individual and the way they treat themselves as well as others treat them.

The purpose of the questions is that I want you to see that just because a person has a rough life doesn't mean they can't change! I have been through more than what I have actually told you!

See, people have a problem! They label other people that they don't even know! Which really isn't fair! I'm sure that you have had that happen to you, and I'm also sure that you didn't like it!

There is also another topic that I would like to chat about. That is ... how we as Americans can just sit on our butts and watch people suffer and do nothing about it! It's truly pitiful! I guarantee that if we tried to help each other instead of feeling sorry for each other, then we would have a better world to live in.

As I see it, we are teaching the right things, but only to people that we know. We have to reach out to people that we don't know as well. For instance, say that there is a child in your son's / daughter's class that you don't want them hanging around because that child look dirty, doesn't make good grades, or even for the fact that they cause problems at home and can't deal with them. So, if you are teaching your child the right things, then you should let your child reach out and maybe help someone else! No child causes problems for the fun of it, he or she is taught problems. In other words, if I go steal from someone, somehow I have been around people who steal, and they have taught me how to steal! See, the point is that we can make a difference to other people who don't have anyone. Everyone in this world is your brother and sister. We have to try.

Even though I didn't have a family to help me, I had a good friend to help me. She, her husband and kids were and still are always there to help me when I need to be lifted up and given a push to go on! All because they care and don't only care about themselves. They care about the world we live in! There are people out there worse off than me and need someone to lift them up and push them to go on with life! We need more people like my friend and her family! That's why I wrote this passage! I beg you to please care and show you care! The children and adults of America need you! I'm not saying to go and take everyone in your home. Help at least one person.

A problem that I had is when I see a homeless person I always thought they weren't anything but alcoholics and I didn't want them to spend money that I gave them on beer or whiskey. But you can help them in many ways! Not with just money! Take them to church, feed them, give them some clean clothes, let them take a bath and try to find them a job. If you're saying to yourself that you wouldn't take them to church or anywhere else because they look bad or smell bad, then you need to go to church more often yourself. Besides, they are your brother or sister!

All I'm saying is get off your butts and show that you love your world.

Meghan and Sherry

a place to start

Tangi still faces the possibility of confrontation on her way to school, no one knows where Raymond Jr. is, and LaTosha and Michael are scared. They watched a man murdered for six dollars in their courtyard two floors below. They heard him beg for his life. They closed the curtains and tried to hide. LaToya doesn't want to play outside anymore. Her friend was killed by a stray bullet. LaToya told her to run, but she didn't listen.

Cheryl, Joe and Cori's mother, sent her oldest son to the juvenile detention center. He had refused to respect his parents' authority. Cheryl transfered the right to discipline her son to an authority she hoped he would obey. She had lost control and was afraid that without immediate action, her son might lose control too. Cheryl wanted to protect him, to teach him respect and to scare him. She forced him to deal with the consequences, this time, before the consequences killed him and affected her other children.

These children are in crisis. Their crises include the despair that exists on the streets, the violence that invades their neighborhoods, the drugs that threaten their youth and the inadequate opportunities that inhibit their potential. Their struggle is constant.

Homeless children and those living in intolerable conditions are straddling a fence. They need direction, guidance and hope. They need to believe in something, develop a vision, see a future. Without these essential elements, their worlds will remain isolated and dangerous. They need intervention.

Dr. JoeAnn Ballard, the director of the Neighborhood Christian Center, is familiar with the obstacles children face. She understands the issues and finds solutions. Dr. Ballard defines disadvantaged persons, those at risk, in her 1986 book, _Serving in the City:_

"The disadvantaged person is one who is deprived and underprivileged. More specifically, he lacks such basic resources as standard housing, medical and educational facilities, and the civil rights believed to be necessary for an equal position in society."

Dr. Ballard wants more people to notice their neighbors, address the issues and offer solutions.

"Look at everybody around you, wherever you are. When you see something that calls for action, do what is needed. Don't spend time on things that do not matter."

Observation is the first step toward increasing understanding. Karen Barber, the past director of Final Net/ The Homeless Children's Program, observed a yearly increase in the number of homeless children standing in line for Memphis's annual Beale Street Thanksgiving dinner. She also observed children living in dilapidated conditions in the inner-city. Final Net was Barber's attempt to respond to the needs of these homeless, previously homeless and disadvantaged children:

"To break the cycle of homelessness and poverty, homeless children must be exposed to and partici-pate in a different world than the one in which they live. They must be given the opportunity to meet caring people of different backgrounds and professions, who can plant seeds of promise and hope— seeds that enable these kids to envision life beyond homelessness and poverty. We feel that all chil-dren can be helped. You don't have to form an agency and save the world, but if everyone would make the effort to make a difference in the life of just one child, we could solve our problems."

There are many ways to enhance the lives of children. We can feed them, clothe them, guide them, comfort them, stimulate them, challenge them. We can share our knowledge, talents and skills. We can encourage them to share theirs. We can listen to their fears, hold their hands or show them a different way.

Tangi shares her fears and hopes with a "big sister"; Tamika turns to a computer teacher; a University of Memphis volunteer helps Sherry with her spelling; Gregory creates artwork with donated supplies; LaToya gets needed hugs from the women of the Junior League; and Joe has seen Cat Country at the new Memphis Zoo. Osha, Stephanie and Terri count on Tuesday night tutoring.

The opportunities for intervention are endless. All we need is a place to start:

Books:

There Are No Children Here, by Alex Kotlowitz; Doubleday, New York, 1991.
How To Save The Children, by Amy Hatkoff and Karen Kelly Klopp; Fireside Book,
Simon & Schuster, 1992.

Local, Regional, and National Resources

Volunteer Center of Memphis   (901) 458-3288
    —various opportunities to fit any schedule

Children's Defense Fund   (202) 628-8787
    —Washington, D.C.-based child-advocacy program

Final Net/Homeless Children's Program   (901) 526-8228
    —tutoring, activities and programs for homeless and inner-city children

MIFA (Metropolitan Inter-Faith Association)   (901) 527-0208
    —provides various services for homeless children and their families

Big Brothers/Big Sisters (Memphis based)   (901) 327-4279

Girls Incorporated   (901) 523-0217
    —Memphis-based program focusing attention on the special
      needs of teen-age girls

Boys Club of Memphis   (901) 278-2947
    —professional guidance for boys ages 7-17

Neighborhood Christian Center   (901) 452-6701
    —tutoring programs for low-income children at various sites

Bethany Home   (901) 525-1837
    —mentoring program for pregnant teens

The Parenting Center of Memphis   (901) 452-3830
    —educational opportunities for parents

Young Women Striving For Excellence   (901) 327-1785
    —volunteer opportunities available to support programs
       for girls ages 7 to 26 to teach them appropriate life skills

Family Link   (901) 725-6911
    —runaway shelter, provides services for children ages 13-17 and their families

Porter Leath Children's Center (Sarah's Place)   (901) 577-2500
    —provides temporary shelter and emergency programs for children

National Coalition for the Homeless   (202) 755-1372
    —provides informaiton on federal issues and upcoming events

Help one Student to Succeed (HOSTS)   (800) 833-4678
    —national groups operating mentoring programs that teach
       children reading, writing, vocabulary, and life and study skills

These children hope for the future, for themselves and for the other invisible children. They want to be seen, understood and encouraged. They want to live long enough to put out fires, build bridges and dance.

All of us who participated in the production of this book—and there were many—share a common belief in the inherent strength of the human spirit. Faced with insurmountable obstacles, most children display an amazing resiliency and determination. However, without encouragement, without the small successes that keep us all trodding along, these children will lose heart. They will not have the strength to lead themselves and those who follow into a less hostile, more enlightened future.

Our cities, neighborhoods and homes are being violated by the escalating rate of violence and drugs. Drive-by shootings, crack houses and children killing children are all too common occurrences. These destructive influences must be overpowered by the spirit and determination of individuals willing to fight back. In order for the children to survive, all of us must come to know them.

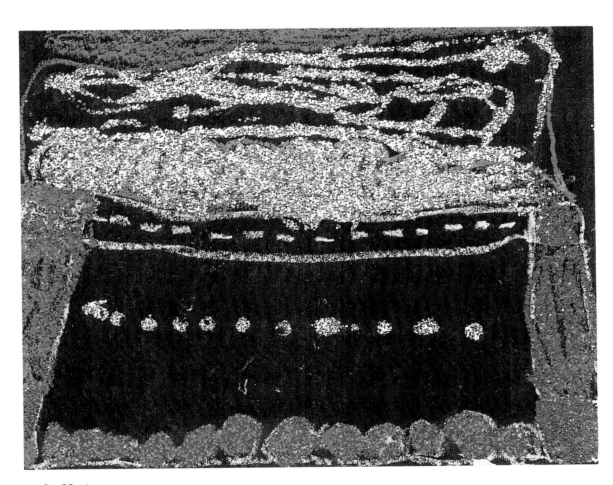

art by Mario

A note from Kathy Kjar

One early Saturday morning while walking in my neighborhood, I came upon a man and young boy playing catch on the lawn. Their throws matched my walk, casual and noncompetitive. As I passed by, their neighbor drove into her driveway. She got out of her car and headed straight toward the man and boy.

"Get off my grass and out of my yard!" she said, as the three of us looked up in shock and disbelief. Realizing that the man was only a few feet on her side of the grass, I was dumbfounded as to what this neighbor had done to elicit such rude treatment. The woman made such a fuss that the man and boy stopped their throwing and went inside. I felt ill when I realized the reason for her behavior probably lay in racial bias.

I tell this story because it happened during the beginning stages of this book. This was the first time I had volunteered to work with children living in the projects of inner-city Memphis. While my family was worried for my safety, my concern was how the children would respond to me. Since the majority of inner-city Memphians are black, would my being white and living in an upper-class suburb be a barrier in this project? How would the children's parents react to me? Would they be like the neighbor and tell me to get out of their communities? Would they tell me to go home?

After a few activities, I forgot my misgivings. I became attached to these children. My camera equipment became the center of attention. "Take my picture!" they would say as they innocently smiled and stuck rabbit-ear fingers behind their friends' heads.

Then they realized the fun of picture-taking and wanted to try it on their own. After brief instructions—"Don't drop it !"—the kids took turns with my equipment and began to see the world from a new perspective through the lens of a camera.

At the time, Metropolitan Inner-Faith Association (MIFA) had started Memphis Imprints, a project in which photographers took homeless children around the city and taught them to take pictures. I jumped at the chance to get involved and teamed up with Steve Cutler, one of my instructors at the University of Memphis. The project culminated in an exhibit at a local mall, with a few photos featured in one of MIFA's publications.

As the months went by, I made many friends. In fact, a very reliable source told me that one boy was going to marry me when he grew up, and a beautiful girl reached up one day with a huge hug and the sweetest kiss. One mother added a note on a T-shirt the children had signed and presented it at the opening of the photography exhibit: "A little time makes a lot of difference. Thank you." I cherish these moments and so many others.

Every venture into the Memphis projects proved memorable. As I would step out of a car or off our bus with thousands of dollars of camera equipment hanging from my shoulder, I became a modern-day Pied Piper. I will never forget being pushed against a fence with ten to fifteen children staring at me, asking to get their pictures taken. The response from the parents was sometimes guarded, but warm and friendly as well.

Valuable lessons were learned from this experience. Simply put, a little effort goes a long way, and whatever I gave, I received much more in return.

A note from Paula Greenberg

Children are naturally drawn to art as a form of self-expression. The visual arts help children react to the things they see and feel. In addition, the visual arts allow children to communicate their emotions, feelings and insights through a variety of materials.

As an art teacher for more than twelve years, I have had the opportunity to work with children from a wide variety of socio-economic backgrounds. In 1990, I moved from New Orleans to Memphis and became art instructor at the Solomon Schechter Day School. It was through my position there that I met Hillari Sasse.

Hillari and a young friend from Houston High School visited a fourth grade class to help them better understand the difficulties and experiences of homeless children in their community. Not long after that, Hillari approached me to do a series of art workshops with the children involved in this book. I gratefully accepted and developed the workshop themes. These ranged from designing dream houses, city scenes and portraits to constructing Matisse-inspired collages dealing with the subject of happiness. Throughout this book, you have seen artwork created during these workshops.

I am grateful to have been a part of this project and to have worked with and been touched by these very special children and the many caring people trying to make a difference.

T H E
GUILD
BINDERY
PRESS